What the Great Depression of 1929–1939 Meant to Me

What the Great Depression of 1929–1939 Meant to Me

Charles M. Armstrong

VANTAGE PRESS
New York

FIRST EDITION

Published by Vantage Press, Inc.
516 West 34th Street, New York, New York 10001

Manufactured in the United States of America
ISBN: 0-533-09585-9

0 9 8 7 6 5 4 3 2 1

Contents

Foreword   *vii*

One. 1930 Economics   1
Two. Marriage   13
Three. The Evening Discussion Groups   17
Four. Social Security   19
Five. My Work with Statistics   23
Six. Trying to Solve the Unemployment Problem   29
Seven. Speculation in the Depression   33

Foreword

I am writing this because I have an urge to clarify my thinking and because the period was a thrilling one. It stimulated my thinking and made some peculiarities of our system apparent. I am not writing it for any particular audience, although I would be pleased if it avoided the rubbish piles until my great-grandchildren have a chance to see it. One of them might be interested.

If we enter another period of economic chaos, like the 1930s, the following comments may be of interest because the underlying reasons for the chaos will probably be similar even though the apparent reasons seem completely separate. The underlying reason for trouble, then and in the future, is likely to be errors, faults in our economic system. The profit system (capitalism) has been very successful, but few people seem to realize the way it has been modified by centralized controls (big government, big corporations, big unions). A very common fault is excessive debt. It was an important factor in 1930 and is at present. Now for the personal story of my part in the great adventure.

What the Great Depression of 1929–1939 Meant to Me

ONE
1930 Economics

First, I would like to say that I was fascinated by the problems of economics, even when I was in high school. I had my first course in economics in 1920 as a senior in high school. While still in high school, I read Babson's book on how to speculate in the commodity markets, and as a freshman in college, I read and admired Adam Smith's *Wealth of Nations.*

My first remembered contact with the great problems of the 1930s was in writing an essay in freshman English in 1921 on the difficulty of paying the war debts. Even then I realized that to pay international debts you had to ship goods, and this is psychologically difficult. Twenty-five years later, toward the end of World War Two, I remembered my freshman essay, which suggested using the funds in each country to stimulate education, and as a result I wrote my congressman. My letter went in the Congressional Record and I think it helped create the thinking that ultimately resulted in the Fulbright fellowships.

In 1925 I went to work in the General Electric Business Training Program. By 1928 I was summarizing business forecasts in the office of the chief statistician. I remember a report in that year from the Babson Service, printed in red for emphasis, warning of trouble, pointing out that there was too much debt. Meanwhile the Harvard Business Service and Prof. Irving Fisher of Yale were saying everything was okay. I believed Babson. (Babson remained a respected advisor. The Harvard Service was dropped.) In August of 1929 I noticed some peculiarities in the orders received at General Electric, and I wrote a letter to my superiors calling attention to a coming change, to less optimism.

(I will make a diversion here to say that I think the 1987 stock market crash should have ushered in a return to reality, but clever operations on the part of the Federal Reserve maintained the optimism. We have been on a long inflation cycle for fifty years and what the Federal Reserve did was to extend the inflation. Inflation will ultimately have to end, and the longer it goes on the harder the ultimate adjustment will be.)

Some things happened in 1929 that should have warned everyone of trouble ahead. President Hoover had won the 1928 election and had promised to raise tariffs to protect the working people. As I remember it, one thousand economists petitioned him not to do it. At the same time, he had a program to stimulate exports. He also insisted on repayment of the war debts of England and France. He apparently did not recognize that the only way large international debts can be liquidated is by shipping goods, and American labor and business wanted the protection of high tariffs to prevent the shipment of goods. England was a proud country and it tried to pay in spite of the barriers. In my view the serious deflationary forces started then as England tried to mobilize funds to pay the U.S.

(Apparently we learn very slowly from experience. We advanced large sums to the Third World in the oil crisis of the 1970s and expected them to repay the debts by shipping us goods, but we have not made it easy for them to sell the goods. We are repeating the mistakes of the 1920s. If the loans had been efficiently used to improve the productive power of the nations involved, the countries could probably have repaid, but they seem to have been used for creating temporary prosperity or sometimes have been wasted in graft. The persistent tendency of all societies is to extend credit unwisely, and when this happens, there is ultimately a time of trouble.)

The optimism in 1929 was omniscient. I was eating in a boardinghouse at that time, and we had interesting discussions at the table. I remember saying that the market price of General Electric stock was too high, and one of the other men at the table said it was unpatriotic to say that the market was too high. The arguments had been so strong that when I came in for dinner on the day of the big crash, everyone laughed. They knew I would be thrilled at the crash.

I thought everything was improving in 1930 and early 1931. I remember buying General Motors stock in July of 1931 at $12 and selling it in November for $16. I also remember going home to East Lansing in August 1931 and discussing with my father the price he should ask for our home there. I agreed with him that he should hold it for $10,000. There was a $6,000 mortgage on it. I returned to the General Electric job, and in September, I talked with the company treasurer and he explained the dangerous condition of the banks. President Hoover, toward the end of September 1931, proposed a plan to save the banks. It was only about one-tenth of the amount needed. I wrote my father in October telling him that I thought he had better just give the house to the bank, if they would take it in payment of the mortgage. This shows how rapidly one's estimate of economic conditions can change.

One of the great lessons I learned in 1929–1930 was

that the determining forces may seem stable for years, and suddenly a new force enters the equation, and the new force may dominate for a period. The usual indices of future trends were overwhelmed by the developing credit crisis. The failure to recognize this resulted in the failure of the Harvard Business Service. Credit depends on confidence, and confidence, when established, almost always leads to overconfidence. With overconfidence banks extend too much credit and many businesses operate with inadequate reserves. In 1929 stock was purchased on a 10 percent margin; in 1989 many corporations were borrowing almost all their working capital. Automobiles were being purchased on five-year credit, and many individuals have since borrowed as much as they can pay for if they have no periods of unemployment or unexpected expenses. So-called junk bonds have been substituted for stock, and many companies are now in danger of bankruptcy.

One of the dangers in the 1989 behavior is what trapped people in the 1930s. Some people think they will invest funds and borrow money at a lower rate than the anticipated return on the investment. For instance, a home owner may carry a large mortgage on his house and then use his savings to buy securities. His assets offset his indebtedness. If some unexpected change in the economic system impairs his investment, he may lose his house. If he had used his money to pay off his mortgage, he would have been secure in his home. The point is that in a complex society one can have extensive wealth in a form that does not give the person the security of controlling even a place to sleep. Ownership is so fragmented that at the same time one may be hungry, one may not have the right to produce food. The pioneers of yesterday could eat if they had the health to plant and care for crops. The modern person may own nothing completely but shares in owning many things. The complexity has made the individual in our society almost as helpless as an individual in a communist society.

In the early 1930s I used my vacations to visit family members in Michigan. I think it must have been in 1930 that I visited my aunt Adelaide Armstrong, in Hillsdale. She had owned stock in a local bank for many years. I suggested to her that U.S. Steel preferred stock would be a safer investment. She went to the bank to see if she could sell the stock and the banker told her that a correspondent bank in Toledo had closed and she couldn't sell her bank stock. She was lucky; she lost her bank investment but did not have to pay any indemnity. At that time a bank stockholder was held to double indemnity.

In 1929–1930 there was a lot of discussion about using construction as an economic stabilizer. The heavy electrical industry was very cyclical. As a result, I explored the possibility of encouraging the utilities to expand in slack times. I found that it would cost a utility at least 10 percent of the construction cost to build a plant one year ahead of need. If utilities were to join in a stabilization plan, someone would have to put up the 10 percent. If prices were lowered, the cost would fall on the producer and stabilization might occur.

According to the economics that I had in college, the usual effect of unemployment was lower wages, lower profits, lower prices. This automatically provided for the desired stabilization, i.e., the reemployment of the unemployed. When I said to some of my coworkers that General Electric should lower wages, they said I should be thrown out the window. No one likes to have their wages reduced.

It was not surprising that there was much public support of the view, advanced by Gerard Swope, president

5

of General Electric, that it was unfair competition to sell for less than the cost of production. With costs figured on the basis of usual historical cost-accounting principles, the result of this philosophy was no reduction of prices in the deflation. The philosophy was incorporated into national policy under the National Recovery Act (the NRA). In my view this philosophy was a major element in the length and seriousness of the Depression. It was to me a serious violation of Adam Smith's ideas. It represented the growing sentiment against the profit system that had in the past brought us prosperity.

In fact, as a result of puzzling over the problem, I developed an alternative cost-accounting system, as logical as the accepted system, that would result in variable prices. The idea involved recognizing that a plant is only fully utilized during prosperous periods and cost charges should only be entered for the part of the plant used at each stage of the cycle. I wrote up the idea and it was published in the *New York Times-Annalist.*

My thinking resulted in another idea that I still think has merit. The unemployed in 1930 were barely existing. If they would work and accept as pay enough cash for bare living and take the rest in non-transferable bonds, they could undertake major developments, like the electrification of the New York Central Railroad between New York City and Albany. If prosperity returned, they would have had their living through the bad period and would be able to liquidate their bonds and have a big savings account. I succeeded in getting the idea considered by bankers in Boston and by Owen D. Young, then chairman of General Electric. About that time President Hoover came out with the Reconstruction Finance Corporation, which many people thought would accomplish the job. President

Hoover's ideas were a step in the right direction but were inadequate in magnitude.

Early on the Depression I was impressed by the security of the people who had a small amount of land and raised their own food. They produced to consume rather than producing for the market. The difficulty was in the system of exchange. As a matter of fact, the difficulty in the 1930s focused on the medium of exchange. I was attracted to the quantity theory of money. The simple formula $MV=PT$ appealed to me. In the formula, M=money; V=velocity, the times money is used; P=price and T=trade. The formula is obviously true; it merely states the obvious. The problem is to understand the forces behind the truism. In the 1930s, a combination of forces resulted in a reduction of M, money. In our society when confidence is high, credit is used as money. When something pricks the bubble of confidence, credit declines, and this is a real reduction in M. When England scrambled to pay its war debts, it made certain commodity prices fall and this pricked the bubble of confidence. Credit declined and either prices came down or trade slowed. Since there was great resistance to cutting wages and prices, trade had to stop. There was not enough money credit to keep trade moving. The homesteader with a few acres producing his own food did not feel the shock of the decrease in M. But the G.E. worker, who produced a specialty and expected to buy his food with his wages, found himself unemployed.

There were many unemployed, hungry people in Schenectady by 1931. Some of them banded together, and secured some land where they could produce food. The group called themselves the Rotterdam Cooperative. This was a grass roots' effort to take care of themselves. In 1932 Franklin D. Roosevelt was elected president. After his election many new laws were passed. Among them was provision for helping cooperatives. The Rotterdam Cooperative received a grant to provide tractors and tools. The grant required the signature of the governor of the state. The grant was made in the winter to help with spring planting. The governor did not sign the grant until I recruited several employed friends and wrote him. The grant was finally signed in late spring. This almost destroyed the coop. The finishing touch was another new law granting relief to the unemployed. When relief gave those sitting on their porches more than the workers could produce in the coop, the coop was destroyed.

The experience of the Rotterdam Cooperative showed me two truths: First, it is easy to make a process so complicated that delays are inevitable. Second, that it is easy to destroy initiative by providing a living without demanding effort. Easy relief is destructive of initiative.

I continued to be interested in the coop idea. A friend, Fred Sarchet, joined me in another effort. We recruited ten men who wanted to garden and solicited funds from our employed friends. One of the ten men had an old truck and transported the men to the garden. Early in the venture, one of the men fell from the truck and broke his neck. His death threw a pall on the venture but we continued. Someone noticed that restaurants threw away considerable amounts of food that could be used to feed pigs. We bought seventy pigs for the men to feed. I had to go to the relief office and say I owned the pigs or the authorities would have cut the relief payments to the men we were trying to help.

The pig venture was successful. The men collecting garbage from the restaurants were stopped by residents along the way who wanted their garbage collected. The pig venture was developing into a business but the old truck wore out. The men came to me in desperation and I loaned $300 to two men on relief to get a better truck. They ultimately repaid me and developed a substantial garbage-collection business. In fact, they became employers. The small loan was critical for their success. Our society has no satisfactory system of creating employment opportunities. Why should anyone have confidence in two men on relief? Such loans are not always successful.

The idea of cooperatives was a growing attraction to many people at this time, 1932–1933. Wherever businessmen could control prices they did so, and eventually the government even helped them under the National Recovery Act. The consumers naturally tried to fight back. Some of us organized consumer cooperatives. Our first success was in buying coal. The coal merchants in Schenectady had an informal but effective scheme to keep the retail price of coal high. We had a large-enough group to buy a carload of coal and break the price. Then we organized a small coop store. We first operated in the Unitarian church, and this was my first contact with Unitarianism. I have been a Unitarian for more than fifty years now. The store was successful and we ended up with three substantial stores in the Schenectady area. At that time there was a strong socialist cell in Schenectady. They moved in on our coop and took control of two of the three stores and destroyed them by poor management. One store survived for many years.

We moved to the Albany area in 1941 and I joined an Albany coop store. We had trouble managing it successfully and finally got a former Atlantic & Pacific store employee who was able to make it successful enough to survive. There was a communist cell in Albany and they moved in on us. They were strong enough (had enough members) to take control. They felt that the old A & P employee didn't have the right spirit and fired him, hiring instead a young man with the right coop spirit. He was a thief and the store failed because of poor management. When it closed no one even knew who the stockholders were. Of course there was nothing left to pay them with anyway. That was the last of my active participation in the coop movement.

The high-water mark for the coop (production for use) movement was the epic campaign of Upton Sinclair for governor of California in 1934. At first, President Roosevelt endorsed Upton Sinclair as the Democratic candidate. Later he reversed his position. Upton Sinclair was a socialist and his proposal carried a threat to established businesses. There is a real conflict between the unemployed and the employed. The Epic Program proposed by Upton Sinclair recognized the conflict and proposed to use state funds to provide the necessary equipment for the unemployed to produce food, clothing, and shelter for themselves rather than giving them cash relief. This used the theory that if regular business could not employ people, the state should employ them to produce their own living.

The result of this thinking is that if regular business cannot provide work for all, it should lose the business of the unemployed. This appealed to me as being fair. Why should businessmen be allowed to hoard machinery? To maintain idle machinery was contrary to Adam Smith's theory of capitalism. It was the development of Gerard Swope's (president of G.E.) ideas, culminating in the NRA idea, which offered real relief for the businessmen. Cash relief is not supported because it is best for the unemployed but because it is good for the businessmen.

Cash relief means that the government pays cash which the unemployed use to buy from the businessmen. It also means that the government often has a deficit, which is inflationary. About this time the Keynesian economic theories became popular. The theory was that

10

FOUR
Social Security

In the early stages of the Roosevelt years, the problem of old-age pensions became important. At that time it was common for children to support aging parents. My brother and I were supporting our parents and accepted the responsibility as proper. With unemployment at 15 percent, many families were unable to take care of elderly parents.

A few corporations provided pensions at that time. General Electric had a pension plan, and part of my job was to supervise the calculation of the pension liability. Gerard Swope, the president of General Electric at that time, was called in as consultant on setting up a national plan, and I, as the G.E. specialist on pensions, was used as a source of information. As a result, I knew that the plans involved a national proposal imitating the private plans. The private plans, including the G.E. plan, assumed that special funds would be set aside each year an employee worked and that these would accumulate and provide a pension at a designated age (sixty-five or seventy). The G.E. plan also provided pensions if a worker became disabled before retirement age. The plan was somewhat like a savings plan where each worker saved something each year. The result was that these private pension plans had substantial reserves which had to be invested. The G.E. plan required a reserve of about $60 million in the 1930s. If one had a national plan, the reserves would be tremendous. I was aware that the problem of investing $60 million safely in 1934 was difficult.

In thinking about the national reserve problem, I realized that there were no good investments unless one had a continually operating society. In 1934 we didn't seem to have a society that could employ its citizens. The problem of investing the proposed large reserve was serious. On further consideration I realized that the real financial problem old people faced was having something to leave their children. If the old people had valuable property, children would be willing to care for them, provided they thought they would get the property. Then I went a step further in my thinking. On a national scale, the real security is in the ongoing society. If it is traditional that each generation is given a living in old age, then the promise is enough to keep each young generation supporting its old generation. Obviously the old generation must expect their support will be a minor load on the young generation. (Social Security payments in 1989 were probably too high for their permanent acceptance by the younger generation.)

I prepared a short memo expressing my fears of the huge reserve and my thoughts on the possibility of operating a national pension plan without the reserves required by private plans. I mailed copies of my memo to twenty selected members of Congress. I received no response. Two years later I received a letter from Professor Cabot, a Harvard professor, asking if I would come to a meeting at Harvard and enlarge on the ideas in my letter which had been inserted in the Congressional Record. Of course I said yes, and started work on my enlarged report. When I got to the meeting I found that Professor Cabot's group were second-level executives (vice presidents) of a number of large firms in the northeast. I also found that among the other speakers on the program was the former governor of New Hampshire, a Mr. Winant, currently head of the Social Security system and its actuary. I also found out that my memo had changed the opinion of the Advisory Council to Congress.

My talk was well received and Professor Cabot had one thousand copies sent out to important people nationally. I later heard that at a convention of actuaries, five had mentioned my paper. The *New York Herald Tribune*, at that time a leading New York City newspaper, printed extensive extracts from my paper on the editorial page. It was a thrilling experience.

As a result of the discussion, the Social Security system was changed and I benefitted by being included under the new low-reserves plan. The original plan would have made it impossible to include people who had not paid into the reserve. Of course a reserve is required for fluctuations in population age groups. The no-reserve idea assumes a constant birthrate. At present, due to fluctuation in the birthrate, the Social Security system is accumulating a big reserve. The reserve is being invested in the government deficit, which is just a burden on the next generation. This supports the validity of my old argument.

It is also interesting to observe that private pension plans have been adopted by many corporations and unions. The result is that the funds have reached such levels that they are hard to invest wisely. They are driving stock prices to what I think will be excessive levels.

FIVE
My Work with Statistics

I had originally thought that I would limit these memories to the economics of the Depression, but as I reviewed my perspective on economics, I realized that my statistical experiences had an important impact on my economic view. As a result, I am going back to pick up some significant statistical experiences. As a junior in college in 1924, I took a course in statistics with Professor Emmons. He introduced me to a new idea that had been developed by Dr. Shewhart of American Telephone and Telegraph in 1923. The new idea was factory statistical quality control.

When I joined General Electric in 1925, I was excited about the idea and talked about it. At one point I was given the opportunity of talking about it with the vice president in charge of research. He gave me a problem concerning experiments with transformer steel. I did well enough with the problem to create a little reputation for myself in statistics. A couple of years later I was assigned to a refrigerator problem. G.E. had been producing refrigerators for three years and they wanted an estimate of their life expectancy. They had a record of the refrigerators built during these three years, including when any had been returned as defective. (As the refrigerator was a sealed unit, all defective machines were returned.) One of the principles of statistics is that you must have a pattern, a regularity, in order to make a projection, i.e., to forecast the life of the refrigerator. Naturally the first step was to test for regularity. One could allow for chance irregularities, but the data had nonchance irregularities and I could not make a projection. I worried about it for a month and asked the machine room (the data was on Hollerith [IBM] cards) for a retabulation. They said they could not give me what I wanted because the cards were sorted for another purpose. We finally agreed on their giving me a broken tabulation (preserving their other sort of the cards). Much to my surprise the other sort provided regularity, and when I questioned the machine room I found the other sort was date of sale. My difficulty had been a wrong perspective. At that time refrigerator sales were highly seasonal so that refrigerators manufactured in the fall were in the warehouse till spring and had no opportunity to fail.

This experience taught me that perspective was very important. It was an extremely valuable lesson that has served me well over the years. It was the key to my previously reported success in recognizing the problem of pension reserves. It was an element in recognizing the developing crisis in 1929–1933. In fact, one of the critical factors in successful stock market speculation is to secure a different perspective than that of the normal, average investor.

I think it was in 1936 that I had another opportunity to try out my quality control ideas. At that time the Warren Telechron Clock factory (a G.E. subsidiary) was having epidemics of sticking and rattling. I was given the opportunity to see if my ideas would help. I had never worked in a factory and I was uncertain how to start. But I was fortunate in having the support of the top management. When I asked that they measure each part of one hundred clocks, it was done immediately. I checked the resulting frequency distributions against the engineering specifications and found that the main bearing holes sometimes exceeded the specifications. I took my findings to the chief engineer and he said, "Impossible." The bearing holes were made by a reamer. This was ground down to the upper engineering limit and everyone knows that a reamer wears down with use. The engineer checked and found that with the particular metals used, the reamer on occasion picked up metal and got bigger. I learned a lesson. Never assume that what everyone knows is true. In one day I had found the trouble.

This started the use of statistical quality control in General Electric Apparatus divisions. Someone else started it in the lamp divisions. I continued to work at Warren Telechron Clock for some time and helped solve other problems.

Two events resulted that were interesting. Mr. Warren of Warren Telechron Clock was a sponsor for a two-week summer program at Wellesley College. I was told to attend for a week at the company's expense and I thoroughly enjoyed it. There were many interesting people there. The meetings focused on the problem of war and the principal speakers were leading pacifists from England. That was the period of Chamberlain and "Peace in Our Time," when young men in England said they would not fight. President Roosevelt was urging the building of more naval ships, and one evening session was devoted to a discussion of the reasonableness of his proposal. The group was overwhelmingly pacifist and against the proposal, so I was asked to be on the panel leading the discussion. I was there to give it a little balance.

Early on in the discussion a member of the panel said, "Who can imagine an army invading the U.S.?" I responded that many in the room remembered an invading army in 1912, Pancho Villa. He invaded the U.S. with about ten thousand men, and if we hadn't had an army, we would have suffered. It wrecked the discussion from the pacifist point of view. It was of interest in showing the way opinion opposed war in the early years of Hitler's threat. Years later, the day Paris fell, I wondered if there would be any way of keeping Hitler from invading the U.S.

I also remember the day in 1941 when the Japanese bombed Pearl Harbor. My reaction was relief that the Japanese had ended our indecision. We were a united country and we were already preparing.

I had another experience worth recording while working at Warren Telechron. The Warren Telechron Clock factory was at Framingham, Massachusetts, which is near Wellesley, the headquarters of the Babson Investment Service. I was driving by the Babson headquarters one noon and on an impulse decided to stop. I wanted to work on the problem of unemployment, how to put people back to work. I thought the Babson organization might be working on it.

I went in and asked at the information desk if I could see someone from the personnel office. The girl at the information desk looked astonished but called personnel. After I had talked a little while, the personnel representative said he would like to have me meet their president, Mr. Pulman. While in the president's office, Mr. Babson came in and I met Mr. Babson, the author of the book on speculation that I read while in high school.

I thought the venture quite a success, and the next day I got a call. Would I like to talk to Mr. Babson? Of course I would, so I made an appointment for my next noon hour. I went to Mr. Babson's office and he was late. He was apologetic and suggested that I come home with him for lunch. I had a family lunch and talked with Mr. Babson for an hour afterward. People sometimes waited days to talk with Mr. Babson. I could have had a job with the Babson organization, but they were not working on the problem of unemployment. It would not have achieved my purpose. The episode did show the power of ideas. Actually, as I look back on my life, I earned my living by having new ideas. The fundamental truths I learned from my statistics helped me toward developing new ideas. Those fundamental truths are worth repeating: (1) Try to look at the problem from a new and unorthodox view; (2) never assume that generally accepted ideas are always true.

I was successfully establishing statistical quality control, but I thought it was logical work for engineers and that my future in it would be limited. Besides, I wanted to work on the problem of unemployment.

SIX
Trying to Solve the Unemployment Problem

In 1937 I decided that my future at G.E. didn't attract me. I wanted to work on the problem of unemployment. The state was organizing an employment service in response to a new law creating unemployment insurance. The new service was to include a research division, and I assumed it would be studying the problem of employment. I took the exam for associate statistician and secured the job. The offices were in New York City. We sold our home on Dean Street in Schenectady and moved to Dobbs Ferry so I could commute into our offices near Grand Central. I was disappointed to find that the research was in paying benefits rather than problems of employment.

After a year in New York City the offices were moved to Albany and we moved back to Schenectady and our friends there. We rented a nice house on Regent Street and lived there several years. While living on Regent Street our second daughter, Nancy, was born and Marion's sister, Gene, was married to William Bradford. Since we were renting, I realized that we had no capability of maintaining ourselves if society should disintegrate into chaos, as seemed possible at that time. I decided to purchase land so we could produce our own living if we had to. I purchased a one-hundred-acre farm with a livable house and a usable barn for $2000 and rented it for $20 a month to people on relief. This covered taxes and a little more. I enjoyed cutting wood for the fireplace and just spending time there.

One of the interesting episodes that resulted was that I advanced funds to buy livestock and had to go to the Welfare people and say I owned the livestock or it would have been taken before further welfare payments were made. Another interesting by-product was that years later, after the war was over, a former tenant called to let me know he was buying a few acres and building a house on the old farm land.

In 1940 our expenses were running too high and we moved to a flat in Schenectady. In July 1941 I recognized that serious inflation was near and that we should own a house. We finally bought a house at 74 Jordan Boulevard in Delmar, a suburb of Albany. We lived there for more than thirty years, and our daughters went to grade school and high school there. We had paid $8500 for the house and later sold it, in 1973, for $37,000. It was not our dream house but we came to love it.

At the time, 1941, I was still working in the Division of Research of the State Employment Service. My work was somewhat more interesting than trying to solve the problems of paying benefits. Washington wanted reports on the labor market. The Depression was over, and Washington was worried about mobilizing workers to produce lend-lease materials to send to Russia and England. I had the pleasure of being invited to speak at the annual meeting at Lake Placid of the vocational teachers of New York State. In that speech I was able to tell them that they no longer needed to worry about where their graduates would work but rather that they needed to worry about getting more graduates. The U.S. was definitely mobilizing well before the attack on Pearl Harbor.

With the attack on Pearl Harbor, we entered the war and there were shortages. Gasoline was rationed and I could not get any to go out to the farm. So I sold the farm to a man who wanted to avoid the draft. I had paid $2000 for it and sold it for $2000, but I had sold $1200 worth of moulding sand also so it was a successful investment.

SEVEN

Speculation in the Depression

A depression is a good time to speculate. It is relatively safe because if the depression ends, you will gain a lot; and if the depression continues, your money will probably lose its value anyway. In other words, if you invest with care, you are almost certain to gain in comparison with the alternatives. The problem is to know when the critical turning points occur. I was reasonably successful, but I made some mistakes. I was also limited by the small amount I had to invest. I started speculating in July 1931. I bought a few shares and in the fall I realized that I had invested too soon. I sold my shares at a small profit.

When I married Marion, she had a little money. I wanted to be cautious with it, and I invested in New York Central Railroad and Pennsylvania Railroad bonds at about $60, as I remember. They went down to, I think, $30, but I held on and eventually sold them at a modest profit (about $400). I had received a good interest return in addition, so the investment was not too bad.

At the time of the bank holiday in March 1933, I had $1200 available, but President Roosevelt was saying he was going to balance the budget. If he did, I thought the Depression would get worse and I didn't invest anything. By May I recognized that he was not balancing the budget and I used about $500 to buy several low-priced stocks. I sold them in June, doubling my investment. A little later I reinvested and again doubled my money. I always considered 100 percent doubling a worthwhile profit. I remember another investment later in the Depression. I had bought a bond of the Steven's Hotel in Chicago. It was in receivership, and I made a good profit.

When the Depression ended in 1941, I bought a house for $8500, which we sold thirty years later for $37,000. Also about that time I asked my wife if she would agree to my taking a $300 loan on my life insurance to buy some very low-priced bonds in a transcontinental railroad. I recognized that Hitler was sinking transatlantic shipping, and I reasoned that ships in coastal shipping, from the west coast to the east coast, would be diverted to transatlantic shipping, throwing a lot of freight on the transcontinental railroads. I was correct, and by 1943 my $300 investment was worth $1200.

I decided to sell my transcontinental bonds, and I used $600 to pay off the insurance loan and reduce the house mortgage. That left $600 which I felt was free for further speculation. I picked out several stocks that looked attractive. When I looked them up in Moody's Industrials, none appealed to me. The book fell open at a company I had never heard of—U.S. Foil. It was a family holding company for Reynolds Metals. Reynolds Metals had built an aluminum refinery, then had start-up trouble and nearly failed. Now, in 1943, it was successful but had a poor reputation. I found the situation attractive and bought 130 shares at about $5 a share. I held the shares for eleven years and sold most of them for $20,000. It provided funds for my daughters' college educations. It was my most profitable stock speculation.